HOLLYWOOD
AN EPIC PRODUCTION

By
William Park

GSD

*GSD
Productions*

Copyright © 2003–2020 by William Park

All rights reserved. No part of this book may be reproduced or transmitted in any form or by any means whatsoever, including photocopying, recording or by any information storage and retrieval system, without written permission from the publisher.

Publisher: GSD Productions

ISBN 978-1-0879-3226-2

1 3 5 7 9 10 8 6 4 2

Cover Motto

Far from Titanic Gloria Stuart stares,
On left, Frank Tuttle, prior to HUAC cares,
On right Carrillos, judge and actor son,
The Technicolor camera soon to run.
Macdonald-Wright from Synchromism's call,
Abstraction left to paint upon this wall,
A realistic motion picture scene,
Where art and science wed upon the screen.

Cover:

Stanton Macdonald-Wright,
Mural for the Santa Monica Public Library:
Moving Picture Industry, 1934.
Oil on plywood panel, 118 1/8 x 113 5/8 in.
Smithsonian American Art Museum,
Washington, D.C. Transfer from the City of Santa
Monica, California.

To the memory of

Alan Downer, James L. Clifford,
and Wilford Leach

TABLE OF CONTENTS

INTRODUCTION 13

CANTO I: BEGINNINGS 21

CANTO II: THE TEENS 29

CANTO III: THE TWENTIES 37

CANTO IV: PRE-CODE 45

CANTO V: INNOCENCE 53

CANTO VI: THE CLASSICAL MOMENT 63

CANTO VII: HOLLYWOOD GOES TO WAR ... 73

CANTO VIII: FILM NOIR 81

CANTO IX: DECLINE AND GLORY 91

CANTO X: THE SIXTIES 103

CANTO XI: THE POLICE STATE 113

CANTO XII: CENTURY AND MILLENNIUM .. 123

FOREWORD

William Park's Hollywood: An Epic Production seduces us without seeming to notice, as only the very best movies can. It leads us - in rhymed couplets, no less - on a steeplechase that cross-cuts all of film history. Blessed with verbal wit and abundant cultural insight, this treatment of a century's collective movie dreams is as easy to consume as popcorn during your first matinee. The fast-moving poem also makes an utterly serious and original contribution to the scholarship of film.

The Poetic Muse, blessed with her gift for lyrical compression and radical jump-cuts, appears to be the perfect historian for our age's essential art form. With a light touch, a questing mischievousness and an encyclopedic knowledge, Hollywood: An Epic Production shows its Swiftian restlessness. This courses just beneath a surface as beguiling as the lost dimpled beauty of Busby Berkeley's prettiest unnamed chorine. Park offers us proof that, when it comes to cross-pollinating genres, the mock-heroic epics of Alexander Pope and celluloid's gaudy pageant of advances and declines can form an improbably perfect partnership. Hollywood, without quite knowing it needed one, has found its informed and playful bard. William Park presents himself as an art-and-industry's Homeric memory, one able to relate the hugest of national sagas in a mere 124 pages. There is nothing ponderous or stodgy in this work; it is as deeply felt as it is richly researched. We immediately sense ourselves in the company of a scholar who is still successfully disguised to himself as the popcorn-loving kid always on the front row, the one whose eyes, forever locked on-screen, have stayed huge with need, belief, with faith in that god-like flame-bright form.

-Lovers of poetry and every movie nut who prides himself on knowing that film trivia is anything but trivial, will all rejoice in the eerie completeness of these couplets, their ticket-holder's glee at all they seek to save. Hollywood: An Epic Production is a moral tale, a four star cliffhanger, an essential act of scholarship and love.

Allan Gurganus
Author of Oldest Living Confederate Widow Tells All

INTRODUCTION

In the early 70s I wrote a book entitled "Hooray for Hollywood." A young editor from the New American Library accepted this for publication and within a day I had an agent. The next week, a senior editor at New American, the husband of one of my students, rejected the manuscript, and my new agent upon hearing the news dropped me. Stunned by this near success, I turned to my colleague Dale Harris and asked him to read the ms. and give me some advice. The advice, kindly given: rewrite it.

Being naturally lazy and having other projects and duties, I laid the book aside. Then for ten years I stopped teaching film history altogether. But when I returned to film, encouraged by my colleague Gilberto Perez, I decided to have another go at "Hooray for Hollywood." I made its rewrite and completion the chief aim of a sabbatical year. As soon as I retired to the garret that served as my study and began to write, something very strange took place. Like Millamant in The Way of the World, who used only billet-doux in verse to curl her hair, I realized that mere prose would not do. Love letters should be in verse, and so should my love, despite all, for Hollywood. So, I began experimenting in rhyme, free verse in the modern mode being far beyond my limited powers.

At first I wrote in doggerel, but when that proved too undignified, I switched to iambic pentameter, to heroic couplets, in the manner of Alexander Pope. And from here, the poetry developed into a mock epic in twelve cantos.

I first encountered heroic couplets in a course in eighteenth-century literature that was then a prerequisite for sophomores desiring to major in English. James Thorpe, the professor, turned the task of introducing Alexander Pope to another teacher, John Weld. When I heard him reading from *The Rape of the Lock*, I wondered how a grown man could devote himself to such drivel. Little did I realize that as Sarah Lawrence's professor of eighteenth-century literature, I would be carrying on for John - he was the only professor at Princeton who insisted we call him by his first name. Much less did I realize that forty-five years later, I myself would attempt a mock epic. There's no doubt that heroic couplets are an acquired taste, but anyone who truly loves poetry will eventually acquire it. Hopefully, for some this poem will speed up the process.

I have dedicated the book to the three men who most influenced the evolution of this poem. Alan Downer, a great and inspiring teacher, was my advisor at Princeton. He taught me how to see the structure of plays, and from him I learned to appreciate the role of conventions in any dramatic art. As he concluded his modern drama course with a film, Tol'able David (1921), I had hopes of writing my senior thesis on a film topic, namely the Marx Brothers. But as either Professor Downer or the Department did not think film or the Brothers Marx an acceptable project, I ended up writing about American stage comedy instead. Ironically, in 1966 when I co-founded film study at Sarah Lawrence, Professor Downer founded it at Princeton. He lived on University Place, in the same house in which in the 1870s my orphaned grandfather was raised by his uncle. When my mother came from Miami for my graduation, Professor Downer invited her to stay with him in her father's childhood home.

James L. Clifford was my advisor at Columbia. I went to Columbia, on Professor Downer's advice ("four years at Princeton is perhaps one year too many") to study drama with Joseph Wood Krutch. But in the interval of the Korean War, in which I served, Professor Krutch moved to Arizona and took up nature writing. His successors, however brilliant, alarmed me, and I decided that the only real mensch on the Columbia faculty was Professor Clifford, the eighteenth-century man. I had loved the works of Jonathan Swift from the first day I read them, but I still had not acquired a love for Pope. Professor Clifford, true to my hunch, saw me through the Ph.D. and helped me secure my position at Sarah Lawrence.

He was the type of the benevolent man who appears in Pope's Moral Essays.

Wilford Leach taught theater at Sarah Lawrence. He later became the first artistic director of the New York Shakespeare Festival and on Broadway won two Tony awards as best director. In his theater course he included a component on film, but he complained that the students were "reinventing the wheel" because of their ignorance of film history. He thought they could learn a great deal and speed up their own development if they became familiar with Griffith, Chaplin, and Keaton, for starters. Gathering from many lunch table discussions that I was a movie "buff," he asked me if I would join with him in offering a film course, one that would combine film making with film history. I jumped at the prospect, and in 1966 we jointly offered, "The Movies, " a one-year course. He was as generous as he was brilliant.

To each of these three men, I owe much of my career in literature and film. With great love I have dedicated this poem to their memory, flattering myself into thinking they would enjoy it, and that they would encourage me to offer it to you, my readers.

HOLLYWOOD
AN EPIC PRODUCTION

CANTO I: Beginnings

    Of Hollywood I sing, and ask thy aid,
O Muse who ever Pope and Swift obeyed:
Fit subject for satire and moral scorn,
Yet source of wit, our age's greatest form,
Where cheap and vulgar profit motives strive
With grace and art, whose glories still survive;
Where petty men, giant egotists hold sway,
Who sometimes block, who sometimes pave art's way;
Mankind in small, writ large for all unfurled,
The glory, jest, and muddle of the world!
Say then, O Muse, how we can comprehend,
This moral, aesthetic mix from start to end.
  As God from evil ever brings forth good,
So from a quaking land he raised up Hollywood.
In latter days with providential ease,
He led the monks to found Los Angeles.
From Olivera's creek to San Pedro,
A modern city soon began to grow,
Four hundred thousand plus by 1910,
With tracks and trolleys, oil and water men,
Where sunlight shines three hundred days a year,

Where oranges bloom, where snow-capped mounts appear,
Where palm trees grow, and ocean forms a shore,
Whose beauties far surpass the lands of yore,
A perfect clime, a land of milk and honey,
Where gringos, goys, and gangsters could make money.
  When from the east, from France, a new invention,
The Fréres Lumière had puzzled out projection.
The man of light, Tom Edison, had seen,
The film, the lens, the spool, but not the screen.
He only saw a box, a little toy,
A peep show penny gadget for a boy.
The more communal French thought that not right,
"Voilà!" they cried, reversed the flow of light,
And from the box where Yankees had to lean,
They shot the frame o'erhead onto a screen,
And now one could attend with all one's friends,
The screening at Salon des Indiennes.
Their workers walked, a train came to a station,
Within two years, it spread to every nation,
The news, the ads, the shots of every day,
The jokes, the tales, the art of Méliès.
A happy public, loyal and never fickle,
Could see all this at noon for just a nickel.
As coins grew high, the lawyers brought them low,
And patent rights drew nigh to stop the show;

But law prevailed and Trusts that should not be,
Themselves fell prey to Fox and Carl Laemmle.
As David slew Goliath, giant of old,
Whose sword, whose spear, whose helm, whose shield tenfold,
Could not withstand the smallest Jewish pebble,
So modern goys could not resist the rebel.
From furs, from gloves, from tacky carny shows,
These sons of David proved too mighty foes.
Or did they rise because the laws were just,
Those laws devised by those who made the Trust?
Or did their love to dramatize their plight,
Plus native chutzpah aid them in their fight?
Or were they chosen, given extra brains,
To civilize the gentile through their pains?
Who knows the cause? The facts we see with ease;
They proved the best; they proved they best could please.
The snobby WASP who kept them out of steel
Could not resist the lucre of the reel;
With nose held high, he lent the "Jew" the dough,
Pleased with himself and profits from the show.
So Zukor, Laemmle, Lubin, Lasky, Lowe,
With Schenck, Fox, Goldfish, Mayer, old Selznick's foe,
They worked together, fought, then joined or wooed,
Combined, dissolved, rejoined, upset, and sued,
And just as God from chaos order brings,

So chosen sons became the movie kings,
And out of strife devised their own empire,
Where they could rule and satisfy desire,
To rise in state, get rich, yet do their part,
To raise with them the state of filmdom's art.

   Before the west, New York had prime of place;
The Great White Way supplied the actor's face.
Production soared, and Porter earned his name.
He taught the rest to cut the fragile frame.
But none so great, who lowly joined the staff,
And gave immortal fame to Biograph.
On Fourteenth Street, uptown, in 1908,}
He came, he saw, he made the crew create}
The art of film, unknown before that date.}
With Bitzer, Pickford, Gish and Barrymore,
His films were such as never seen before.
Close-ups, cross cuts, with angled shots and pans,
He broke the stage, brought drama to the fans.
Who was this man with heart and mind so keen,
Another Abe but born to free the screen?
The art no doubt he raised to higher place,
But fell himself before the curse of race.
D.W. Griffith, greatest name is he!
Forever tainted, shame of Liberty!

   He knew his art two reels could not fulfill

And left New York, went west, and joined DeMille,
The first to use a set where oranges stood,
A farm it was, and known as Hollywood.
As David sinned but could regain the Ark,
His namesake with the middle name of Wark,
Could also triumph, give the town new fame,
But fall himself, and ne'er repent his shame.
He saw the light, he felt the inspiration,
To write in light the history of the nation.
From Hollywood to Chatham Griffith went,
To build the sets, to stage the great event:
Of charge, attack, of flags in cannon's mouth,
Of death, "War's Peace," the ruin of the South.
Still more, alas! the faithful recreation
Of that "Great Heart's," of Abe's assassination.
All this so true, so good, and yet a lie,
Because it was so smeared with bigotry.
No nation can be born with such a plan;
No nation can be saved by Ku Klux Klan.
Alarmed, amazed when censorships arise,
He turns and builds a tower to the skies
Of Babylon of old to make the claim,
INTOLERANCE alone deserved the blame.
Yet courts decreed that film was not an art,
And First Amendment rights could not impart

Protection to a business so commercial.
The lesson learned: avoid the controversial.
For many years the lonely towers stand,
Yet he himself forsook the troubled land,
Took **WAY DOWN EAST** and **ORPHANS OF THE STORM**,
Back to New York where he controlled the form.
An artist, yes, but business sense he lacked,
And loss of funds made him smart Zukor's hack.
He wished Gish well, sent her to MGM,
And turned to drink and died without a friend.
The genius crushed by cruel Hollywood?
The artist's struggle vainly to do good?
Or self-destructive Puritan's demise,
Who from young girls could not avert his eyes?
Or did time cool the ardent artist's rage,
A victim of changed mores and old age?
  So Hollywood began its tangled story
Of race, of laws, of bucks and art and glory,
At once a place of vice and hate and schemes,
At once the home of highest human dreams.

CANTO II: The Teens

   Farewell New York! the port of migrants' plight,
You couldn't compete with California's light.
The stage you had, the fame, the banks, the fans,
But not clear skies and ever-sunny lands,
Where lots were cheap, unspoiled like nature's jewels,
Where hands were cheap, unknown to union rules.
At first the little independent crews
Sought out the light and high Pacific views,
But soon legits, from rain and freezing breeze,
Themselves took train, took stars, took companies.
   Westward they came, those corp'rate pioneers,
Whose names now gone are lost to later years:
> American, Beauty, Eclair, Domino,
> Komic, Kriterion, Bison, Broncho;
> Kaybee and Essanay, Alco and Kalem,
> Owners initials, the letters would fail them,
> Royal and Princess, Rex and Majestic,
> What noble names for products domestic!
> Then Nestor and Victor, Sterling, Reliance,
> Too many to live, they needed alliance.

As larger fish upon the tiny feed,

And sharks upon the large impose their need,
So smaller firms to middle came about,
When lo, they fell a prey to Paramount.
They struggle to survive but all in vain;
What good the film without a theater chain?
What good the chain without a booking man,
Who guaranteed delivery in a can?
From out the height of starry mount's logo,
From where wise Zukor oversaw the show,
He first to do what others did in starts,}
He took control of all three business parts,}
And set the stage for future movie arts.}
So too did Fox who in his New York lair,
Saw Marcus Loew combine with L.B. Mayer,
And Brothers Warner Vitagraph obtain,
And to First Nat'nal fix their family name.
To these big four we should add Universal,
Where Stroheim worked, the madman of rehearsal,
Which from small IMP a studio became,
Though Laemmle failed to buy a theater chain.

 Now as the dust of commerce settles down,
Appear the stars who first won world renown.
Not Sweet, not Marsh, but Pickford crowned the queen,
The fav'rite female sweetheart of the screen.
Her hair of gold, her tears, her zest, her pluck,

Her drive to turn bad chance into good luck,
Amidst a time of war and darkest night,
She fought the odds and opened up some light.
Miss Norman came from Keystone with the Kops,
With breakneck speed and laughter without stops,
She couldn't arrest the faster habit's harm,
Despite Mack Sennett's love and zany charm,
And break the curse of drug's dependent need;
She died too soon like younger Wallace Reid.
Then Fatty at the top of laughter stood,
Until that day when banned by Hollywood
Because Virginia Rappe had somehow died,
And he was blamed, set free, though three times tried,
But not before the censors rose in spleen,
And bade Will Hayes to bowdlerize the screen.
   It was an age of energy and art,
Of dashing Doug and cowboy Billy Hart;
The one with smiles and acrobatic grace,
With flips and leaps and earth defying space,
Amazed the world and showed the movie fan,
An all-Amer'can optimistic man;
Not so the other, gloomily he rode
From good to bad and bore the moral load,
Or bad to good he struggled back again,
But paid the toll, out West where men were men.

As stars grow hot, expand, contract, and die,
So stars once bright recede from public eye.
The life of fame survives but just a day,
As comp'nies fail and films in cans decay.
We know the names of stars like Pearl White,
But who has seen her Pauline's valiant fight?
A FOOL THERE WAS lives on in paper print,
So Theda Bara breathes to give a hint,
Of how frail men fell helpless to her vamp,
So shocking then, today it looks like camp.
The paper prints but served the Patents' Trust,
And when it died, a film could turn to dust,
Or better still, when slightly out of date,
Recycled was, the silver from nitrate.
So film escaped from narrow copy laws,
To be chewed up by time's commercial jaws;
And Theda's later work and looks to kill,
If left at all are left upon a still.

  But as Greek plays defied the odds of age
And trod once more upon the modern stage,
Some movies too by chance have been redeemed
And can again be seen upon the screen.
To these we add the sum not just the part
Of all of Griffith at the Modern Art.
We see the female growth of child-like Gish,

Perplexed by love, o'erwhelmed by passion's wish.
We see the rise of Bobby Harron's star,
Shot down, by chance? before he got that far.
From out this troop, the seeds of talent poured:
Barthelmess, Crisp, Von Stroheim, Walsh, John Ford.
  But none have earned immortal fame so well,
As Cockney kid who climbed from childhood Hell,
Onto the stage, Fred Karno's featured clown,
Whose drunken dance broke sober houses down.
To Keystone, Sennett, Hollywood he came,
Assur'd he could become a star again.
At first he played a cad, a lady's menace,
But then the crew encamped and went to Venice,
To film the kids at soap box auto race,
Where he amused the crowd and made a face,
As cars rolled down, came quickly off the ramp,
Upon the lens the camera saw - The Tramp!
Big shoes, small vest, bag pants, moustache and cane,
A waddling walk, a hat that tips in vain,
A comic role that worldwide fans adored,
A comic role for forty years explored.
He did it all, but not without some aid;
His loyal crew were patient, overpaid,
'Til Rollie rolled his camera, keeping pace,
And Edna smiled and gave the dream a face.

Of all the comic artists and their means,
None better knew the paradox of screens:
That empty space should fill and action gain,
As motion moved within a rigid frame.
In rings, in rinks, on sands, in homes and stores,
In slums, up steps, and through revolving doors,
The more we saw, the more we loved his face;
The more he ran, the more he stayed in place.
As waiter, migrant, convict, cop, or swell;
As miner trapped in Yukon's frozen Hell;
As soldier, father, fireman, tipsy, tight;
As bum whose love restores the blind girl's sight;
As fact'ry hand beset by all that's new,
THE GREAT DICTATOR countered by a Jew;
A humane mix of laughter, tears, romance,
A perfect blend of picture, mime, and dance.
He stands before me, looks into that bar,
I see his back, the cane, the door ajar!
I see the rose, the smile, the face;
The screen fades out before such God-like grace.
Like Homer, Dante, Shakespeare unsurpassed,
So Charlie Chaplin's art will ever last.

CANTO III: The Twenties

   Speak not of whopper hits and Midas stars,
Of tube and channel network, VCRs!
The twenties were for film the golden age,
And all the nation moviedom amazed.
One hundred mil the population stood,
And ninety mil each week went Hollywood.
From one to two, from two to eight the reels,
The films got big; the stars got sex appeals.
Victorian curls cut off for Flapper bobs,
And flaring nostrils gathered in the mobs.
   What Europe lost in war to ne'er regain,
As shattered comp'nies failed to rise again,
Unable to compete with Hollywood,
Whose profits mounted, never higher stood;
Yet Hollywood's success grew not from gold,
But from its point of view, then new and bold,
The common man's perspective, plight and dream,
And stooping rose to dominate the screen.
As raindrops fall but to the creeks converge,
And creeks to streams that with the ocean merge,
So drawn by force of wealth and art and fame,

The springs of talent flowed and westward came.
The nati'nal town hemmed in by mount and sea,
Became the world's prime picture colony,
Whose native light already shone afar,
But gained new luster from the foreign star.
Chaplin, Jannings, Laurel among the men;
Little Mary Pickford - Canadienne!
Whose fickle fans preferred another face,
And flawless, quiv'ring Garbo took her place.
With Negri, Lubitsch journeyed from Berlin;
Yet greatest German star was Rin Tin Tin,
The smartest dog that e'er on screen appeared,
Whose looks, whose stunts, whose mind the crowd endeared.
Not stars alone, directors, technics come,
Hans Dreier, Murnau, Stiller and Seastrom.
Just as the Pilgrim migrant made the States,
And native born the migrant tolerates,
So Hollywood that stands for U.S.A.,
Owed its success to migrant come to stay.
   And now arose on Universal lot,
A set to match the Continental plot
Of **FOOLISH WIVES** by Stroheim well devised,
As Monte Carlo loomed before Van Nuys.
The tender loves of country girls and boys
Gave way to more sophisticated joys,

To naughtiness, seduction innocent,
A game of love that ridiculed consent,
Where men betrayed and women suffered much,
Until revenged by wit and Lubitsch touch.
  Onto these screens in shimm'ring silver glow,
Gigantic actors dwarfed the fans below,
While music from the organ or the pit,
Aroused the soul and to the action fit.
Here Garbo and John Gilbert torrid prove,
While Gish sinks down to die of cold and love;
Here Frederick stirs the ashes of her fire,
And pays the price of freedom and desire.
Now Valentino condescends to flirt
In Gaucho pants and hat and open shirt.
The Russian EAGLE, Arab SHEIK he plays,
And decent women lust for matinees.
As profits rose reality declined,
And far-away and make-believe aligned.
In costume drama daring Doug beclad,
As ZORRO, PIRATE, ROBIN, or BAGHDAD,
And ancient stones the camera tracks bestir,
As team of black attempts to spill BEN HUR.
More sacred yet the sacred pages bring,
The TEN COMMANDMENTS, even Christ the King,
And censors struggle ever more in vain

To stem the flood of sacred and profane.
   More mundane films could also set aglow,
The fans of Swanson, Talmadge, Clara Bow,
The working girls who guaranteed a hit,
If El'nor Glyn decreed them full of "It."
For younger fans, for boys, old men, and hicks,
Pranced forth proud Tony, mount of Thomas Mix.
Or Fritz, least known of all film's fav'rite steeds,
Who galloped o'er the land in TUMBLEWEEDS.
For adult themes, so called, one looked in vain,
Unless one saw them in the anguished pain
Expressed in masks, by fearful hidden graces,
Those masks of Chaney and his thousand faces.
   Not lost, not known beyond the local scene,
Apprenticed here the future of the screen.
John Ford to Harry Carey added thrills,
While Capra Langdon lent his writing skills.
McCarey, Stevens, Hawks, still unassayed,
When Vidor rose to make THE BIG PARADE.
That Farewell Scene! As trucks move to the right,
And René seeks out Gilbert in her fright,
And holds his leg, this man whom she adores,
A leg soon lost in carnage of the wars.
This film made Vidor, Gilbert, Metro proud,
And spite of gloom, they let him film THE CROWD.

Between these peaks he could with Davies play,
A Davies much maligned since her hey-day,
A comic talent none then thought the worst,
Because she was the "girl" of Rancher Hearst.
King then progressed to still another height,
And all Black HALLELUJAH! brought to light.
  But best of all, the Twenties' comic part,
Which raised low slapstick to immortal art,
And greatest critic, never failing time,
Bestows the laur'l upon the clowns of mime.
Above the rest, beyond mere accolade,
The Tramp had slowed, four pictures only made.
To rival him an acrobat stage star,
Revealed in film a talent on his par.
Two reelers, yet within the flicker's spool,
Unwound the laws of Newton, Nature's rule,
As Buster leaps to see-saw on a fence,
What threatens him he turns to his defense,
And gravity that forces most to fall,
He demonstrates can liberate us all.
Ladders, pulleys, slides, and railroad track,
He saves THE GENERAL, brings his sweetheart back.
No avalanche, no stream, no storm, stampede,
Can that sad face with spinnng legs impede.
But ten short years was he allowed to run,

By friends, by drink, by M.G.M. undone.
Not so the awkward boy of sheepish grin,
Whose lovelorn antics n'er a girl could win,
Until he gathered strength from untapped source,
And triumphed over men and natural force.
A human fly, he climbed up faulty wall;
A human shot, he ran, outran the ball;
A comic art of shame, embarrassment,
Though pants, though coat, though pockets, sleeves are rent,
He dances on, determined to the end,
That hidden tailor, tacky suit can mend.
When bomb blew off his hand, he wouldn't succumb;
The public laughed and Lloyd was number one.
Langdon, Chase, there were so many stars,
Yet none endured so long as those TWO TARS.
While Ollie upward looked, Stan scratched his head;
How could so odd a couple share a bed?
SONS OF THE DESERT leave their family cares,
Mae Busch back home awaits them unawares.
At home, at work, with dates, with wife and gun,
They blundered still and maddened Finlayson.
If trees they sold, or grand pianos shoved,
The more they wrecked, the more they were beloved.
When comedy was king, invention ruled;
It set free space, and time itself it fooled.

And now the store, the local op'ry hall,
The vaudeville stage could not encompass all.
For this new art, new space was in demand,
And movie palace rose throughout the land.
Ornate and gilded, built in all the styles,
Baroque, Egyptian, Roman, Deco piles,
With guardsmen ushers, bronze sculpted doors,
With op'ra stairwells, murals, and marbled floors,
Their likes the public n'er before had seen,
Whose fabled walls enhanced the silver screen.
But few remain, the wreckers' ball tears down,
What once gave art and glory to downtown.
No Roxy, Loew's, or Paramount compete,
Yet reigns Olympia still on Flagler Street,
And Chinese splendor, showman Sid Grauman's,
Still pavement fame imprints to mortal hands.

CANTO IV: *Pre-Code*

   What shattered Jazz Age dreams of easy cash?
The falling stocks and bonds, the Market Crash.
No longer college antics, football games,
That symbolized the rising classes' aims;
No longer flirty flappers bashful ploys,
Could snare the genius of the comic boys;
When Jolson sang, and brought the pictures sound,
The talkies gagged on social change profound;
No longer Ruritania's romance ruled;
The public wanted tough guys, coppers fooled.
So when Doug Shearer freed the mike again,
It listened in to little feisty men.
James Cagney reigned with gun, grapefruit in hand;
Distinctive speech the mark of this new brand.
No sooner land a part in Broadway play,
Then off to Hollywood at higher pay.
So Tracy, Muni, Bogie, Rob'son come,
The bosses, rats, the mobs of moviedom.
It's LITTLE CAESAR, SCARFACE, "nation's shame,"
Who massacres dread Karloff's bowling game.
One need not wonder how this change was wrought;

It was not sound that cynicism taught,
But rather stocks and bonds, a market crash,
That shattered Jazz Age dreams of easy cash.

   Such gangsters played for real the power games;
They could not win unless they bossed the dames.
Silk shirts, cigars, of dress clothes they were fond,
But nothing suits so well as hard-boiled blonde.
Blondell and Todd, Harlow and Farrell the best,
All owed their roles to scandalous Mae West.
With hands on hips, with smirks for every fan,
"You can be had, my easy riding man."

   The title gone, talk thrives in this new genre;
Quick wit runs wild and doubles its entendre.
The censors groan and look in stark dismay,
As necklines plunge, and stars risk lingerie.
Lubitsch adapts, shows virtues mixed with vice,
Creates his best, TROUBLE IN PARADISE.
Kay Francis out of love lets Marshall steal;
Hopkins grabs the dough and says it's "real."
Romance? The fans can never get their fill,
But who would guess they'd favor MIN AND BILL?
Dressler and Beery number one become;
THE CHAMP fights on and dies to save his son.

   Ruth Chatterton, Twelvetrees, and Dot MacKaill:
They fall to rise o'er men who always fail.

The men, they die, get sick, or leave the land,
A cripple in his chair?, she'll understand,
Or bully who exploits her through the kid,
She works, endures, reluctant to get rid,
Of male oppression till the final reel,
When death or fame reward her sex appeal.
Thus sacrificing all for family,
She keeps her honor, gains her liberty.
To this new breed, now sighing on the screen,
Arrives "The Kraut," the Dietrich called Marlene.
As Amy Jolly, Lola, Shanghai Lil;
As body curves, unswerving is the will.
Joe casts on her his net of fetish charms,
Unfolds the scene with camera of Lee Garmes.
With darkling plots, lost souls in dim-lit bars,
These were the first, original film noirs.

   A fallen world! Who fights against despair?
Not drunken upper class, not crooked mayor,
Not chief too dumb or in the gangsters' pay,
One man alone, the newsman of the day.
A wise guy rebel, never really bad,
"He's the best reporter we ever had."
"The killer's loose"; the editor goes wild,
Yells, "Stop the press!" and "Find the missing child!"
With hat pushed back, he phones; he types non-stop;

He bluffs, outwits the gang, comes out on top.
For men alone was this brash role confined?
No, leading ladies city rooms refined,
And gals thought doomed as sisters of the sob,
Iconoclastically destroy the mob.

   Not stars alone were lured from off the stage,
But brash young writer Hecht from his FRONT PAGE.
With saucy, snappy, streamlined dialogue,
The boys of Broadway kept the fans agog.
Not least of them Bob Riskin makes his way,
And with Frank Capra joins, O happy day!
These two with Harry Cohn raised Gower Street
From poor man's row to studio elite.
Let PLAT'NUM BLONDE, AMER'CAN MADNESS be!
Shines GEN'RAL YEN from Music Hall marquee.
Columbia lifts high her sacred fire,
As wit with warmth, as form fits with desire.

   With sound the eastern gang saw profits grow,
And Sarnoff, Kennedy formed RKO.
With Selznick, Schoedsack, Cooper put in charge,
KING KONG breaks loose and seeks Fay Wray at large.
Fay wonders, Can this trip be "on the level,"
If raised so high by lovelorn ape, not devil?
They shoot him down; he gropes into the sky;
In Thirties movies, monsters always die,

And Kong like child of giddy FRANKENSTEIN
Must fall to raise a reassuring sign
To those into a deep depression cast
That modern man-made monsters would not last.
   In FREAKS and vampires hope could not be found;
Far greater consolation came in sound.
For then the movie musical was born,
And shapely dancing legs the screen adorn.
The blondes, brunettes, they tap, they smile, they wink;
While photo cell keeps all their lips in synch.
Now singing voices can at last be heard,
And Jolson's joined by Cantor, WHOOPEE's nerd.
As autumn leaves in glorious colors fall,
So westward blew the breeze that brought them all,
And with them seeds of future movie fame,
The likes of which we ne'er shall see again.
Bright Broadway hears the call and like a thief,
Steals off, packs up, and boards the Super Chief.
Wheeler and Woolsey, RIO RITA's nuts,
Go West with Brothers Marx and COCOANUTS.
With Groucho's verbal wit, non sequiturs,
With grande dame Dumont's idiot allures;
With silent Harpo eloquently crazed;
With moron Chico's index finger plays;
Sans Gummo, Zeppo sings and lends some class;

They chase the girls, deflate each pompous ass.
Freedonia calls, and Firefly takes a bow,
And warns, "If you think things are bad right now,"
(Anticipating war when Calhern's hit)
"Wait to ya see when I get through with it."
"Hail Freedonia," insane land of the free,
For peace or war the cure is anarchy.
   As New York gave to Hollywood its plays,
So Hollywood intent on its own ways,
Gave back New York a BROADWAY MELODY,
With its own songs, like "You Were Meant for Me,"
By Herb N. Brown and tunesmith Arthur Freed,
Who destined was e'en Broadway to exceed.
Like films of old the musicals engage
To do no more than imitate the stage,
Until Mamoulian, Ernst Lubitsch arrive;
Their fluid cam'ras bring the screen alive.
Jeannette Macdonald sings with all her charms;
Her naughty looks lure Maurice to her arms;
That Chevalier who bends with hat in hand,
While Berlin, Gershwin, Kern strike up the band.
They write as well for movies as for plays,
And break our hearts with their immortal lays.
Director Berkeley parts from Broadway too,
And brings a new perspective into view.

Instead of fixing cam'ras in the pit,
He shoots above, below, and with his wit,
Turns all the chorines into film design,
And makes new space with image mock-sublime.
A hundred legs become a lustrous star,
Or balls or flowers, violins bizarre.
With roller skates, pianos, water falls,
He edits dance to cinematic laws.
When FORTY-SECOND STREET creates a rage,
From Warners he inherits huge sound stage,
Where Ginger sings Pig Latin without pay,
Lies "ere-way in the oney-may."
As Ruby clumps and Dick Powell's tenor croons,
Golddiggers plot to Warren-Dubin tunes.
FOOTLIGHT PARADE, depression's pains to kill,
Has Cagney hoof on bar with Shanghai Lil.
His sailors march; their placards signal far,
The flag, the N.R.A. and F.D.R.
For Hollywood, in touch with its poor fan,
Could still remember "My Forgotten Man."

CANTO V: Innocence

    The New Deal dealt new hope in Hollywood,
Which stacked the deck in favor of the good.
Then Cagney changed, though still with gun in hand,
He swaggered now, J. Edgar's own G-MAN;
And all those sexy, stoic, fallen girls
Lost out at once to Shirley Temple's curls.
STAND UP AND CHEER the Federal people say,
As CURLY TOP, MISS MARKER lead the way.
If New Deal was expressed by this new mode,
The formal cause was the Production Code.
When sound was heard, Will Hays was hardly seen,
Until his office went to Joseph Breen.
Now scripts could not be shot unless approved,
By moral readers wanting films improved.
    Farewell Mae West, begone double entendre;
Farewell pale flesh, and fallen woman genre.
Hello good priest who blessed with common sense;
Hello child star and age of innocence.
To some this change meant right-wing fascist plot,
Brought on by Mayer, Spellman and that lot.
But such a view means people are but fools,

Not subject to those Samuel Johnson rules:
"The Drama's Laws the Drama's Patrons give,
And those who live to please must please to live."
If fans rejected all that light, those kids,
And sent the movie mogul on the skids,
Then movie mogul who invented Breen,
Would change the code and darken up the screen.
So Shirley, Freddie, Judy, Mick remain,
With Jackie, Gloria, Deanna, Jane,
Bonita, Dickie Moore, and Bobby Breen,
With DEAD END kid determined to come clean;
Alfalfa, Darla, Spanky, with Buckwheat,
The Our Gang Kids who live just down the street.
  With New Deal notes in optimistic key,
The writers swing with screwball comedy.
Frank Capra, Riskin rising to new heights,
In four weeks shot a movie of three nights.
Five Oscars won, appealed to members' hearts,
It was the first to win for comic arts.
Claudette from yacht, from angered dad she flees,
Falls in with Clark, on bus, and sings "Trapeze."
No foil to masher's line "Believe you me!"
She gives a hitchhike lesson: show your knee.
Run-down auto court cabins in a row;
The scene of rope and Walls of Jericho.

Such wit combined with Walker's camera's skills,
Gave Capra fame, gave Harry dollar bills.
While Clark, Claudette enabled it to win,
The film absolved the upper class from sin.
Her dad says "mug"; King Wesley is a "pill";
No need for blood and revolution's kill;
Instead we'll laugh, their antics make us see,
The rich are poor, worse off than you or me.
As marriage ends all struggle over class,
The stuffed shirt sees we're all the same at last.
As class dissolves in love's alembic cup,
The groom or bride will raise the other up.
Not so with race, the Blacks held in reserve,
Unless they sing, or dance, or shine, or serve.
She said she'd rather play than be a maid;
Yet Hattie's Oscar left the debt unpaid.
   Though sexes battled in the end they found,
More lasting love the second time around.
Thus Dunne shows Grant, before too blind to see,
That he's her mate, not foolish Bellamy;
But not until he suffers and feels shame,
Will she allow the "different" to be "same."
THE AWFUL TRUTH, the truth not awful state,
The movies like the Church allow one mate.
Absurd convention? Work of priests and Breen?

Or divine truth revealed by Nazarene?
The Code imposed some silly laws unsound,
But also opened comic depths profound,
For comic code decrees an end of strife,
Where wit restores the love of man and wife.
  New times demand new stars light up the dark,
And Beery's reign succeeds to crown King Clark.
Thus Cooper, Power, Fonda, Stewart, Scott,
With Taylor, Flynn, and Grant control the lot;
Because such looks had ne'er before been seen,
It seemed that WASP alone would rule the screen.
For females looks alone were not enough;
No object of the gaze! These gals were tough.
Reporters, workers, e'en soci'ty dames,
Saw through the men, their puny sexist games:
Large-eyed Bette, with neurotic laugh;
Arthur, mainstay of reportorial staff;
Stanwyck who suffered and seldom had fun;
Arched eyebrow, song, and teeth of Irene Dunne;
Mad wit (foul mouth) the tragic Carol Lombard;
Kate lorded over Ginger, on her guard;
Lupino and Sheridan, Russell, more joy!
Colbert and Young, Sisters Bennett, and Loy.
One need not ask where Suffragettes were seen;
The women's movement marched across the screen.

Poor Fox went down, its assets all on loan,
In need of chief like hated Harry Cohn.
Darryl Zanuck, who favored timely plots,
Warners left to share the Goldwyn lots,
No modest man, his company laid claim,
To all the Century held within its name.
Schenck set the deal to tempt the wonder boy;
He came, he merged, he made the studio goy.
He lost Will Rogers, downed with Wily Post;
Young Shirley rose as favr'ite coast to coast.
The writers' friend, a writer once himself,
The gold of books he changed to movie wealth.
A natural chief, he ruled the lot with ease,
Until destroyed by fatal brain disease.
To you O Muse! we bow in our appeal;
Implore thy aid for words that make us feel,
The greatest glory Thirties movies bear,
The dancing, singing Rogers and Astaire.
As ancient Greek, as wondered modern man,
How Homer could compose his epic span,
So wondered we how in these latter days,
Despite the Crash, the wars, the lethal ways,
An art like Keats's storied Grecian urn,
Again appeared preserved in cam'ra's turn.
From famed screen test: "Can't act, can dance a bit,"

Fred took a plane to Rio, made a hit,
He put his head to Ginger's head, the dunce,
And said, "Let's try this 'Carioca' once."
On patterned floor in black and white they dance,
Perfection in their steps, their arms, their glance;
A chemistry of equal gender love,
A magic mixture sent from high above.
All hail Mark Sandrich, Pandro Berman, wise,
Who understood what passed before their eyes,
Three cheers for Taylor, Dwight, and Alan Scott!
Who gave Bidini, Bates, plus puns and plot.
All praise to dance director Hermes Pan!
To Ginger Fred, to Fred a Ginger man.
The Big White Set designed by Van Polglase?
Or Carrol Clark or workers who amaze?
Rococo, Neo-Classic, Neo-Space,
Still firm foundation for the dancers' grace.
They first transform Cole Porter's DIVORCEE,
Now Fred makes love to Ginger "Night and Day."
He reckons, "Chance ... the Fool's" fond "name for Fate,"
A tragic thought, which proves to have no weight.
Confused Tonetti twists the phrase about,
Till "Fate's no Fool, take a Chance" comes out.
As Horton sings with Grable and knocks knees,
So tragic words transform to comedy's.

Next Fred encounters Ginger, fake chanteuse,
Who's "Hard to Handle" at the Cafe Russe.
She sings her wacky number, then they dance,
The first of many times she's wearing pants.
Though TOP HAT hangs on what is in a name,
It matters not when they're "Caught in the Rain."
So what if Blore leads Rhodes offshore to seek,
When Dale and Jerry, close, "Dance Cheek to Cheek."
In FLEET they stoop, assume a class below,
And in bell-bottoms win as they "Let Go."
Before a mirror Connie changes all,
Forever framed by Grable, Lucille Ball.
Scott says he never writes, e'en to his mom,
"What would I say?" he asks with some aplomb.
"You could tell her you love her," she replies;
"She knows that," he smiles, and blinks his eyes.
Depression's sorrows seem to sink the show,
Yet Bilge risks all and lets Bake raise the dough,
And Berlin's tune reverses fate's advance,
They "Face the Music" once again, and dance.
Next SWINGTIME slowly makes its start,
Then tribute pays to Bill Bojangles' art.
When "Never Gonna Dance" strikes up the beat,
We know the wolf left Fred Astaire his feet.
That double stair! That swell, That belle romance!

With forty takes, they consummate the dance.

Though "They All Laughed," "Change Partners" still to come,

And SHALL WE DANCE? explains the low-brow fun,

As Petrov pitches off his ballet shoes,

And shows that tap can also claim a muse,

The series fades; the form starts to decay;

It will not serve the BARCLAYS OF BROADWAY.

As Vern, Irene, they play their final part,

And dance once more beyond the reach of art.

CANTO VI: The Classical Moment

   As Thirties waned, the films waxed ever bright,
As if to stay the fast approaching night.
Though far removed from Europe's viper's nest,
The troubles of the decade travelled west.
Not just the loss of socialist Sinclair,
To dirty tricks of MGM and Mayer;
More troubling than utopian's wildest dreams,
Were racketeers' and labor unions' schemes.
As moguls took too much of movies' gain,
And treated folks far worse than monarch's reign;
The writers, dupes; the stars, enslavéd hacks;
(Davis herself could not defeat contracts)
So unions rose, Writers,' Directors' Guilds,
In hopes to break the power, cure the ills.
Bitter the fights, as Reds became involved,
Who claimed all good was by collective solved,
Who took just cause and rendered real abuse,
Transforming them for communism's use.
Some good emerged from out the furious fray,
But seeds were sown for studios' fatal day.

    Presiding o'er the strife and labor plots,
Stood L.B. Mayer, leader of the lots.
Roared MGM, and took the lion's share;
Uncanny Thalberg's sense had brought them there.
Wed to Shearer, but cursed with feeble heart,
He lowered others, raised producers' part.
As courts of old upon Versailles took form,
So MGM became the moguls' norm.
There Gable Fletcher Christian incarnates,
While Laughton's Bligh seeks, not in vain, for mates,
And swears he'll Fletcher hang from high yardarm,
Yet Fletcher steers the BOUNTY safe from harm;
While Tone redeemed from guilt and mutiny,
Swears England sweeps the seas for liberty.
So thirties films through troubled oceans yaw,
And favor rebels, yet support the law.
At home Judge Hardy understands his son;
Mister Mayer weeps; Mickey's number one.
In jungle Tarzan swings with Jane his mate,
His primal cries all nature subjugate.
In city suave detectives drink and quarrel;
Yet THIN MAN's caught by Nick and Nora Charles.
In song when Nelson sings "I'm Calling You,"
The fans are sure Jeanette will come in view.
More earthy stuff sounds forth from Harlow's breath,

Until her kidneys poison her to death.
  Each major had its galaxy of stars,
And marquee told the stud'os from afar.
If Temple, Fonda, Don Ameche, Faye,
Or Power, Tierney, Darnell lit the way,
Then Fox's modern logo would be seen,
As deco searchlights scanned above the screen.
If Cagney, Davis, Muni, Powell, or Lanes,
Blondell, Bogart, Ron Reagan, Garfield, Rains,
De Haviland joining hands with Errol Flynn,
Then two big letters and big sounds begin.
If Cooper, Crosby, Colbert, C. DeMille,
Then ring of stars above a pointed hill.
If Hepburn, Rogers, Grant and Fred Astaire,
Great radio tower signals in the air.
This was a world, a cosmos made by art,
Unreal yet real through allegory's part.
It dealt with issues in a thin disguise,
Unseen by critics cursed with lit'ral eyes.
  Two independents scaped the lion's maw,
Goldwyn and L.B.'s own young son-in-law.
Like Polish jokes, Sam's speech was put in doubt,
Though certainly he coined "Include me out!"
Brash David Selznick fled poor RKO,
To found the fief he mastered by memo.

Unlettered one, the other college bred,
They sought the films where taste and profit wed.
From novels DODSWORTH, WUTH'RING HEIGHTS, Sam chose,
From plays, DEAD END, with Lillian Hellman goes;
REAL GLORY, MARCO POLO, HURRICANE;
While Selznick gave us Mrs. Norman Main,
Then ZENDA, SAWYER, INTERMEZZO played,
And bought the book that Margaret Mitchell made.
  A third there rose from obscure drawing board,
In time's vast womb someday to prove a lord;
At first content with cartoon's lowly part,
Amidst the vast expanse of filmdom's art.
When sound arrived, contracted this expanse,
It left a space for cartoons to advance.
Then Disney modeled Mickey, added Duck,
Put color to the pigs and with some luck,
Increased production, formed a studio,
Released his shorts each week through R.K.O.
Yet shorts alone prolonged financial plight,
Until Walt saw the future and SNOW WHITE.
The dwarfs, the drawings, freely moving doves,
"Hi Ho," "Some Day," and Prince with "But One Love,"
Bequeaths a genre to the art of space,
And animated features take their place.
Just as the myths with animals are rife,

Their presence probing mysteries of life:
Are we like them of cyclic nature bred,
Forever doomed to struggle 'till we're dead?
Or do they speak like us so we can know,
That compost earth but clothes a spirit show?
So Disney films, though fashioned for the tyke,
Like Dopey speak to fool and wise alike.
  As Bazin said this was film's classic age,
Where system, genre, stars, montage engage,
And merge into what seems a perfect form
That ever since has served for movies' norm.
Auteurs abound, like Capra, Hawks, and Ford,
Yet hosts of others cannot be ignored.
They minor masterpieces made with ease,
One thinks of Greg LaCava, Mike Curtiz.
MY MAN GODFREY, the butler surnamed Park,
Forgotten Man found slumming, on a lark,
Who leads the foolish rich to find good will,
Create "The Dump," and transform Hooverville.
As Johnny Tarzan shall forever be,
And Karloff's mug in FRANKENSTEIN we see,
As Rathbone has for Holmes, not Watson, stood,
So none shall better Flynn as ROBIN HOOD,
A film more left and populist by far,
Than any dreamed by Russian commissar,

Where all the conflicts of the Thirties meet,
Where upper classes earn their sound defeat,
Where Norman race the Saxons can't suppress,
Where virile man saves maiden in distress,
Where natural king will tyranny repeal,
As F.D.R trumps all with his New Deal.

  Yet writers groan, as glides castrated pen,
Cut off, they think, by falsely moral men;
Yet what a paradox, not understood,
How censorship works for the writer's good;
Not absolute: "Conform or be shot dead!"
Its boundaries serve to stimulate the head.
The Code but banned the gross, the true obscene,
Not from the plot, but only from the screen.
If on the art a blockage so malign,
How then explain the films of '39?
All Hail! GONE WITH THE WIND, Vivien Leigh,
Scarecrow, Tin Man, Lion, and Dorothy;
All classics now beyond banal reproach,
Yet left behind by Ford and Wayne's STAGECOACH.
The list so long, yet each deserves a line:
As YOUNG Abe LINCOLN solves the heinous crime;
DRUMS beat ALONG THE MOHAWK, DESTRY RIDES;
Davis goes blind; BEAU GESTE in death confides;
James Stewart croaks to Senate with parched lips;

Alas! the Oscar goes to MR. CHIPS;
DIN blows his horn; ONLY ANGELS HAVE WINGS;
While Cathy calls, NINOTCHKA has her flings;
At last brave Warners takes on NAZI SPY;
While Ginger tries to hide new baby's cry;
And crippled Irene Dunne sings her sad song,
In hopes some day Boyer will come along;
If Tracy seeks a passage to the west,
Paul Muni dies, yet Mexico is blest.

   Fabled age! succeeded by one more,
Whose glories almost match the year before:
With Tracy Lord triumphant Kate returned,
To Hollywood who had her talent spurned;
And woman's man George Cukor proves again,
That he could win awards for able men.
In Wyler's LETTER, Davis sins once more;
A female Hildy won't leave newsmen's floor;
A nameless Joan loves Max in Manderley;
Falls FOREIGN CORRESPONDENT to the sea;
Errol Flynn swings through the rigging as of yore;
Bob Hope and Bing set out for SINGAPORE;
FRANK JAMES returns to win his bitter fight,
As Bogart and Lupino DRIVE BY NIGHT;
While Betty Grable subs for Alice Faye,
And dances up from Argentina's WAY.

For foiling crooks, BANK DICK is given junk;
Powell rhymes, "It's not the coffee it's the bunk";
Carol Landis, Vic Mature with dinos toil,
And Oscar goes at last to KITTY FOYLE.
The Joads roll out on Highway 66;
And Charlie mocks THE GREAT DICTATOR's tricks.
So ends a decade filled with movie lore,
When hate broke loose and movies went to war.

CANTO VII: Hollywood Goes to War

   Halfway, O Muse, on your broad wings I've flown,
Inspire me now, don't leave me on my own.
So small the wit I find within my brain,
So great the subject I would entertain.
For now Pearl Harbor sinks us into war,
Crazed Hitler strikes where he ne'er struck before.
Say then how Hollywood, the land of seems,
Could muster up a force and lend its means,
To wage a war too long kept out of view,
THE BELL, it tolled, it tolled for movies too.
   First then be praised a son whom some deplore,
This, Major Capra, who had served before.
Called by George Marshall, picked by F.D.R.,
To teach the nation "who the heck we are";
To make a group of films called WHY WE FIGHT,
Which showed a world o'erun by Fascist might,
Unless Democracy could turn the tide,
Through strength of arms inspired by mental pride.
The cynics laughed, besmeared "Fort Hollywood,"
Yet F.D.R. approved and deemed them good.
Not for G.I.s, Gyreens, and Swabs alone,

The films were shown at "neighbs" to reach the home,
And those born since must see to understand,
How wartime zeal swept isolation's land.
   While Capra cuts before the giant Steembeck,
The brightest stars eclipse to hit the deck.
James Stewart flies his missions, not for fun;
An older Clark joins up to man his gun;
A young Ty Power shoots for the Marines,
While Fonda, Ford choose blue and ocean scenes.
The others over thirty-five could serve,
With 4-Fs in the Hollywood Reserve.
O mock them not, for serve they did and well,
And kept morale from dropping into Hell.
   In '41 Bob Hope CAUGHT IN THE DRAFT,
BUCK PRIVATES Bud and Lou got their first laugh,
As Andrews Sisters crooned to "Bugle Boy,"
The stars signed up to fight the Nazi ploy.
As usual filmdom's gangsters led the way,
Yet slow at first to take the cut in pay:
Cagney becomes a CAPTAIN OF THE CLOUDS;
While Ladd converts and brings along his pals.
The last hold out, grim Bogie squints his eye,
To war, to love, to song "As Time Goes By."
Unmoved when Ingrid pleads for spouse and cause,
He shrugs, pretends he lives by Vichy's laws,

Till love resumed reveals the Nazi stench,
He rallies, plays the anthem of the French.
With quickened eye he sees the need for war,
And makes the sacrifice he couldn't before.
Undaunted by the Colonel and his threats,
He shoots the swine; then Rains rounds up suspects.
   For fate of Jews and death camps' devilish rage,
The movies wait until a later age.
How much the moguls knew? What were the lies?
A sad debate which to the White House flies.
Though Grant and Rogers taken were for Jews,
The wartime films adopted other views.
   Since face to face we first confronted Japs,
The conflict spread ACROSS...PACIFIC maps.
WAKE ISLAND's gallant stand became a show,
And when it fell BATAAN was sure to go.
The Nurses' Corps SO PROUDLY them WE HAIL;
CRY HAVOC lent an ear to their travail.
AIR FORCE raised up the boys from all the States;
Hey "Brooklyn," "Tex," "Dakota," we're all mates.
We'll fly together heedless of the woe,
Give Spencer Tracy time o'er TOKYO.
Meanwhile Marines like Mitchum, Randolph Scott,
A raid prepare on islands foully got.
When Japs defend Guadalcanal in vain,

The movie Gyreens land and win again.
John Ford on Midway won a purple heart;
On Key Biscayne he won the laurel of art.
The PT men, EXPENDABLE, THEY WERE,
Who slowed the Japs so victory could occur;
A film that rose above the wartime hate,
And eulogized the brave who fell to fate.
  In Europe combat waits till '44,
And D Day's films succeed the end of war.
On cold Atlantic sea the actors fight,
And lead the convoys through the darkest night;
Or make a raid on France's bristling shore,
CRASH DIVE to show the Nazis what's in store.
Airmen escape, no prison can them hold,
And join Resistance women, strong and bold.
SS, Gestapo monsters plot and scheme,
Embodied in that role, Helmut Dantine.
While Stroheim, former "Hun," Rommel conveys,
Dug up, destroyed by Tone in CAIRO's GRAVES.
  From front to front the movie heroes go;
From Europe Grant guides sub to TOKYO.
First Flynn with Reagan 'scapes the Nazi goon,
Then leads through Burmese jungle his platoon;
While Wayne shot down in Paris waits to fly,
His FLYING TIGER clears the Chinese sky.

As Carlson's Raider, Scott the Jap defeats,

While steering corvettes to the U-boat fleets.

A BERLIN CORRESPONDENT at war's start,

D. Andrews in Japan wins PURPLE HEART.

As Pigeon on vile Hitler lines his sights,

His MINIVER in England also fights.

Best travelled Bogie saves our great canal,

Takes merchant ships 'cross NORTH ATLANTIC foul,

Leaves Rick's to fight SAHARA's desert scene,

And ends by cleaning out the Caribbe'n.

   As heroes die to fight the foe again,

Show Biz responds and sends its singing men.

Ameche leaves the band and takes to air,

YOU'LL NE'ER GET RICH drafts dancing Fred Astaire.

George Murphy turns in taps for Army boot;

Desi breaks up his band and learns to shoot.

Irving Berlin, who won the war before,

Enlists again and sings "Get Up" once more.

Powell joined the fleet, left Ruby in the lurch;

Bing Crosby wished to serve but joined the Church.

   On land, on sea, in air, we fought the war,

With bond drive led by Dorothy Lamour;

With U.S.O. and HOLLYWOOD CANTEEN,

Where starlet danced with sailor and marine.

STAGE DOOR CANTEEN, and THANK YOUR LUCKY STARS,

They also served who only stand in bars,
Where Bette Davis sang the truth so bold,
In war the men too young were or too old.
   Just as o'erseas the war struck every day,
So home front epic, SINCE YOU WENT AWAY,
Where Colbert, former nurse, now wife bereft,
Sees Walker, from BATAAN, seek second death,
As Monty Woolley, Temple, Jones all pine,
She buckles down and works the 'ssembly line.
Then Walker strides again in his third life,
Beneath THE CLOCK seeks Judy for his wife.
Pres Sturges HAILs the CONQUERING HERO home,
And Bracken claims the medals not his own.
John Hodiak arrives for SUNDAY meal;
Anne Baxter sings and stirs their sex appeal.
Bob Cummings saves New York from Nazi plot,
Returns from war and falls for Liz'beth Scott.
   Fake stories real emotions as we grieve,
The loss of those who had no screen reprieve;
Or cheer the victors true of that just war,
So ably imaged by the filmy corps.
As in the east the sun will first arise,
Though desert mountains block it from the skies,
The light at last will shine upon L.A.
Turn back the fog and bring resplendent day,

So Hollywood, at furtherest western shore,
Though far removed from either theater's war,
And last to see the daytime's natural light,
Could play its role and circumvent the night.

CANTO VIII: Film Noir

   Explain, O Muse, how changed the movies are;
How could the victors introduce film noir?
How come it is that classic art must go,
Become baroque and then turn rococo?
Explain if noir a style or genre be,
Peer through the shade of time and mystery.
   It all began as much of Hollywood,
Back in New York, where junior Orson stood,
From Merc'ry Theater, Mars, the wonder boy,
Went west to RKO, to him a toy.
He studied Ford, the film that made John Wayne,
Rolled back the stage, came up instead with KANE.
No Mr. Smith to raise the Senate up,
This was a world of innocence corrupt,
Paid off reporters, bosses who can smear,
Success a myth for which one pays too dear.
A Freudian world of deep subjective gloom,
Where parents haunt from birth until the tomb.
As falling leaves invoke the changing times,
And all the birds with sense seek warmer climes,
So Hollywood from Karl to Sigmund turned,

For like old stars, old gurus can be spurned.
From center frame to edge, to dark from light;
From flat to deep, to ceilings short'ning height;
From God-like unobtrusive story track,
To many views, each one with its flashback;
From un-self-conscious seeming plot's unfold,
To voices over, image now controlled;
As Orson draws attention to his tale,
Asserts his art against conventions stale;
From absolute to relative he led,
And left unsolved the mystery of the sled.
   One wonders if young Orson had not seen,
An obscure "B" by Ingster on the screen,
With Lorre as the THIRD FLOOR STRANGER star,
Some critics claim it was the first film noir.
Made just as Welles at RKO appeared,
It conjured many tricks that he revered:
A flashback plot, key lights, and close-up scream,
The shaded face, dark stair, and surreal dream.
It knocked off Lorre with his psycho look,
Redeemed that little punk, Elisha Cook.
Did Musuraca, Wild this style devise,
To open up tired double feature eyes?
Whate'er the reason in this little "B,"
Film noir began as it did end, in parody.

Yet other films lay claim to be a first;
THE MALTESE FALCON, innocent of Hearst,
With private eye, Sam Spade, who peers between,
The dumbbell cops and crooks with minds more keen;
A desp'rate lady seeks a stronger male,
A killer proved, he sends her off to jail.
By Hammett made, by Chandler soon surpassed,
The private eye, ex-cop, with fag and glass,
Whose seedy office, seedy scenes succeed,
With wise cracks, guts, he follows every lead.
Through fog he walks, gets conked on his sore head,
But wakes in time to talk the villain dead.
For Spade and Marlow, Bogie was the pick,
Forever since he's symbolized the dick.
　　From James M. Cain a Billy Wilder play,
Where Barbara Stanwyck puts her spouse away,
With help from Fred, who hides it all from Keyes
Then dictaphones the truth, falls to his knees;
An all too human man too weak for fate,
A sexy, wily dame who needs no mate.
Then MILDRED PIERCE, reversal of this plan,
Where stronger woman gets betrayed by man.
Now gone the equal status, 30s pride;
The sexes' battle ends in homicide.
OUT OF THE PAST means one must live in fear,

From dangerous Kirk and ever-lying Greer.
Mitchum himself must face his double loss,
And pay his dues and die for double cross.
This is a world where Bergman plays the whore,
And Grant, her pimp, can't figure out the score;
Where LAURA's face haunts Andrews as a dream,
Where Tierney's love destroys Webb's self-esteem;
A world of rain-drenched sidewalks, turned up coats,
Of has been drunks and off-shore gambling boats,
Of lonely lamplights, empty streets, dark walks,
Venetian blinds and bucks that bribe the talks;
A world of shades where all the men wear hats,
Where love more lethal proves than gangsters' gats;
The hat-check girl shuts up or gives the tip;
The henchmen bite when hero gives them lip;
The songster sings the blues from nightclub's floor;
The truth awaits behind the boss's door.
Voice over not a choice but hidden rule;
Joe Gillis speaks face down from swimming pool;
And Ed. O'Brien suffers all the way,
Yet tells his tale though he's marked D.O.A.
At lakeside hideout, mountain's purer home,
The guilt, like fog, creeps in; one can't atone.
Except through death and time's devouring maw,
Yet Code persists, and all is framed by law.

So at the end the guilty ones are doomed;
The gov'nor speaks and order is resumed.
The titles spell the world the cameras mark,
And CITY, NIGHT and FEAR align with DARK,
While EVIL, FALL, ALONE recall the PAST,
And SLEEP or SCREAM and NIGHTMARE KILL the cast.
   Some 30s actors fit into the style;
Joan Crawford's face was never more worthwhile;
And crooner Powell turned deaf to music's beat,
Got tough, and nearly croaked from MURDER SWEET.
But different plots now different looks demand;
They gave Palance; they gave us Gloria Grahame.
They gave Malone and Windsor, Janet Leigh,
The victim, Cook, the villain, Dan Duryea;
Winters they gave, so many had their start,
Noir gave Monroe her first important part.
For new directors, actors star-like soar;
Alas, James Dean signs off at twenty-four.
But Douglas, Brando, Lancaster remain,
Bill Holden, Peck, and Mitchum start their reign.
From Granger mild to Heston's sterner stuff,
Noir favored hunks who never got enough:
Stumbling, stoic, they know they're double crossed;
They suffer on, though everything is lost.
Mitchum and Burt and Ryan lead the van,

Mature's in peril, whom Widmark calls "Big Man."
   Directors too in noir make their debut,
Not only Welles, Nick Ray comes into view.
A LONELY PLACE left Bogie without gun,
THEY LIVE BY NIGHT put youngsters on the run.
If LUSTY MEN put rod'os on the screen,
The REBEL caused young stardom for James Dean
Fritz Lang remade Renoir in SCARLET STREET;
Turned Glenn Ford loose to scorch the mob's BIG HEAT.
Siodmak gave Ella Raines whose sultry look,
Inspired the beat of crazy drummer Cook,
And Hemingway's short story he'll rewrite,
As flashbacks show why Swede must die tonight.
Don Siegel snatches bodies in L.A.,
Then lines them up on San Francisco Bay.
Jules Dassin craves the documentary look,
And strips the CITY NAKED for the crook.
Proves Preminger a heavy handed grace,
His SIDEWALK leads to FALLEN ANGEL'S FACE.
Sam Fuller shows why people hate the Reds,
But also shows they're right to fear the Feds.
While Tony Mann began with SIDE STREET scenes,
With Stewart he moved west to wider screens.
Group Theater grads put pictures in the can;
Its greatest triumph: Elia Kazan.

And Kubrick youngest, makes it to this list,
Starts his career by filming KILLER'S KISS.
   While bigger films to Technicolor go,
These little B's proceed to steal the show,
As heaven's star sinks fast in western bay,
Yet brings out light unseen throughout the day,
So black and white in this its final scene,
Makes us lament it no more lights the screen.
Then Garmes and Walker, Daniels, kings of light,
Were joined by Alton, Musuraca, Seitz,
Guffey, Biroc, Cortez, who lit the cast,
And turned to art the newer stock made fast.
   How then explain this world of dark and death?
What force, what cause could give it light and breath?
Perhaps war's sorrow could explain the plight,
Which changed film's love of day to need for night.
As Agamemnon, Trojan War's proud king,
Brought home not peace but guilt to his offspring,
So Allied victors home from a just war,
Could not forget the blood they spilled before,
And like Orestes who the Furies fled,
In nightmares screamed they weren't alive but dead.
Heroes now weak and overwhelmed by doubt,
Run from themselves, can't face what life's about;
Penelope-like women of good will,

Turn Clytaemnestra-like and seek to kill;
So though they brought the Axis to its knees,
Their doing good by evil won't appease.
Or could it be that noir from Europe came,
A gift from Adolph's dirty racial game,
For those who knew how best film noir could please,
Were for the most part German refugees,
Who taught their UFA skills to Hollywood,
And saved the naive Yank from too much good.
   Some say the atom bomb caused the despair,
And others that McCarthy fouled the air;
That leftist writers dealing with their past,
Must justify or testify to last.
Or could film noir be but an outward sign,
Of Hollywood's demise and state of mind?
As TV took its audience away,
And anti-trust decree sped up decay,
As theater, distribution, studio split,
No longer did the empire model fit.
With back lots empty, crowded sound stage bare,
Film noir expressed the end of the affair.
With Freud and flashbacks, voice o'er his grins,
It framed Gene Kelly, Esther Williams' swims;
It fractured Donald, hatched out Daffy Duck,
Gave Capra look to Bailey down on luck;

It wondered whether BEST YEARS were worthwhile,

For post-war years it was the period style.

Just as baroque gave opera its birth,

And rococo delivered novel's mirth,

So from the womb of '40 - '58,

A dark new genre blessed by crime and fate,

Attended at its birth by mid-wife Welles,

His TOUCH OF EVIL tolled its funeral bells.

CANTO IX: Decline and Glory

  The Fifties were the darkest decade yet,
By TV, law, by cold war fears beset,
And politics, long smoldering since the war,
Burst into fires that burned to Congress floor.
As Eve and Adam fell in Milton's "Nine,"
So Hollywood succumbed to scoundrel time.
Look down O Milton! eye this not askance,
Pray Providence inform these rhymes not chance.
  The Left thought they alone the Fascists fought,
And stood for freedom both in art and thought,
And since they had the Nazis first withstood,
Had earned the right to govern Hollywood,
To show the mass how bourgeois was corrupt,
How law a sham designed to cover up.
They thought the Right reactionaries shrill,
Who hated thought, and rather think, would kill;
A mindless, menschless, mean, demeaning lot,
Who in each work of art saw commie plot.
They saw the Lib'rals fall to HUAC games,
And wring their hands, but still turn in the names.
The moguls, whom the Leftists ever dissed,

Could keep their thrones and also keep their list.
As heroes then, the Ten defied the hate,
Of red-neck WASP who Jew and Commie bait,
And went for worthy principles to jail,
Where martyrdom and innocence prevail.
  The Right saw them in diff'rent light,
As Stalin agents serving Soviet might,
Or fellow travelers, dupes of KGB,
Who hated US and all our history,
Into whose scripts, for writers most they were,
They'd slip the words which Rightist crimes infer.
STRANGE LOVE OF MARTHA IVERS a good case,
Of how to use a melodrama's face,
T'indite the rich, expose the comp'ny town,
Unmask the sick and bring the "structure" down.
Film noir, with crime and guilt, despair,
A perfect form to fit the needed fare.
They lied about their past, the present twist,
And sacrifice the truth for Alger Hiss;
A scheming, paranoid, ungrateful lot,
Who hid behind the freedoms they would blot.
  Where then the truth in this forlorn debate,
Which faction made and ripped the land in hate?
To keep a secret list of former ties,
Which might be based on spite or downright lies?

And naming names in State considered free,
Could be the means to end democracy.
Yet if the Left was right, how can one see,
Once prosperous countries turned to beggary?
How then explain the ever-mounting toll,
Of purge and war, of millions on death's roll,
Of promised freedoms locked in prison's gate,
Of brave new world of tyrannizing state.
Though Right, in fear, to vicious tactics went,
The Left, though smeared, was never innocent.

   As studios sank, and Hollywood declined,
The decade offered masterworks sublime.
For then the oldest genre came to life,
Inspired by civil rights and civil strife.
Depression dormant, then waylaid by war,
The cowboys rose and rode the range once more.
Not just Republic, Monogram, the B's,
Not just the Rogers, Hopalongs, Autrys,
But now the major stars, the best auteurs,
Put on sombreros, donned their chaps and spurs.
Ford took the lead, the western he defined,
And made the great MY DARLING CLEMENTINE.
As Aeschylus of old had once devised,
How justice from the lust of blood could rise,
Explained how civil laws and civil state,

Had origins in violence and hate.
So Ford took Tombstone, Earp, OK Corral,
Chihuahua, Clantons, Holiday his pal,
And showed how law and order came to be,
How death and Shakespeare mixed their company,
From rustling, gambling, patriarchal rule,
Came brothers, barbers, churches, and a school.
Alas! the half-breed from the plot dismissed,
As Fonda asks, "What kind of town is this?"
For further trails he now recruited Wayne,
Relieved to wear suspenders once again.
As Kirby Yorke, he joined the cavalry,
At FORT APACHE pondered history.
Ford showed again how delicate the scale,
Which weighs the truth when order must prevail;
As old prospectors fearless as they rode,
Into the hills in search of mother lode,
So Ford the norms of western film explored,
Unearthed the gold amidst conventions stored;
Not just the mesa, Steamboat Rock we see,
Nor horsemanship of Johnson as Tyree,
Nor splendor of the skies and vistas large,
Nor wind-swept hats as horses rear to charge,
Not only scenic splendors here we find,
But also grub to feed the greenhorn mind.

How justify the white man's constant gain,
Against the price of red man's fatal pain?
Displaced by time and space the west could deal
With racial issues undisplaced and real,
As trading posts and reservation flights,
Perspective gave to hate and civil rights.
So BROKEN ARROW pointed up the way,
To two great works, both penned by A. Lemay.
THE SEARCHERS showed a white girl turned to red;
THE UNFORGIVEN red to white instead.
In both a brother makes a forlorn plea;
In both the search leads but to tragedy.
Though whites play reds in casting quite bizarre,
They make a point best seen in SEARCHER's Scar.
His eyes are blue, like half-Comanch John Wayne;
They signify we segregate in vain.
What matters it if mortals are but "other,"
Unless we see that red and white are brother?
The greatest scene in all the west I ween,
Occurred when Debbie ran across the screen,
And brother Martin Christ-like raised his arm,
And stands before mad Ethan's lust for harm.
   Not Ford alone nor Walter Huston's son,
Concerned themselves with how the West was won;
Budd Boetticher teamed up with Randolph Scott,

Went on location, left the movie lot,
And made small westerns, fabulous to see,
Such as COMANCHE STATION, THE TALL T.
Then Mann chose Stewart, or he chose Mann;
They too went west, WINCHESTER in hand,
Shot up the villains, rid the land of slime,
Whose crime it was to mirror Stewart's mind.
And Wyler who had travelled west before,
On larger screen, with even larger score,
Conveyed the conflicts of the east and west,
Of male and female, brother brothers best,
The final duel: a father kills his son.
BIG COUNTRY weeps at how the west was won.
  The second Hepburn rose to charm the fan,
Her girlish love bestowed on older man;
While Hepburn one took Tracy from above,
And as she stooped discovered equal love.
Once ingenue, Miss Hayward's FOOLISH HEART,
Beat strong enough to win an Oscar part.
Minnelli turned the FATHER OF THE BRIDE,
Gave Caron Kelly, Cyd Astaire beside,
With SOME CAME RUNNING featured S. MacLain,
Whose every role was every picture's gain.
Dean Martin far from Lewis Frankie saw,
With Duke and Rick and Hawks upheld the law.

From New York's leftist Group Kazan came west,
Went back to Broadway where he staged the best
Two plays the post-war, pre-war world had seen,
Came back again, put Williams on the screen;
And with his actor Brando braved the mob,
Contender once, who wanted honest job,
Who blew the whistle ON THE WATERFRONT,
Where naming names was more than witches' hunt.
With all that Griffith, Remick, Neal allowed,
He held the mirror up to FACE ... THE CROWD.
  If these to monumental heights arrived,
The art of Alfred Hitchcock also thrived.
By Thirties perfect in his chosen mode,
He too went west to mine the treasure lode,
To dig, explore, reveal the psyche's crime,
Then exorcise the guilt in nick of time.
From Manderley's dark halls and Max he went,
Wherever Selznick's contracts had him sent.
To Holland, LIFEBOATs, small town U.S. scenes,
Nor fame nor wealth could squelch the artist's gleams.
SUSPICION glows as milk in poisoned glass;
And Uncle Charlie preys on upper class,
While Little Charlie thinks of him as king,
Until she shares the secrets of his ring.
And Bruno waits on every passing train,

Almost succeeds in driving Guy insane.
Now Bergman joins the list of glorious blondes,
Of whom some critics say he was too fond;
First as a mom to infantile Greg Peck,
In witty script devised by author Hecht,
Where secret crime through Dali's set revealed,
Serves but to mask the incest kept concealed.
Then on to Rio, so to serve the State;
Blackmailed by Grant to be sick Rains' playmate.
The love of Hitch they say put girls at harm,
Who mutilated, killed, with frosty charm;
Yet in the four great films with this as theme,
We see another, probing, healthy scheme.
Far from misogyny as dark as pitch,
We find the women's friend in Doctor Hitch.
Alicia suffers, yes, but for just cause;
The villain of the piece is Dev, and laws,
Those laws of men who hearts control,
And sacrifice true love for harlot's role.
If women suffer in these films, we see,
The reason is the male voyeur, "It's me!";
The male who cannot love because obsessed,
Afraid of sex, who wants his woman dressed.
So Jimmy Stewart looks from WINDOW REAR,
Projecting onto Burr his sexual fear,

A Burr who saws his nagging wife in hate,
So Stewart, fans, the men, can liberate,
And in these vile psychotic acts may see,
Themselves undressed, stripped down from mystery.
A much more active Stewart Day sedates,
A man who knows too little and too late.
She screams in time above the "Hymn to Joy";
She sings, "What'er will bring" and saves her boy.
Now Stewart falls to nadir of career,
In VERTIGO of heights and love in fear,
As sympathetic Scotty he pursues,
Madeleine, Carlotta, and museum views.
But when he draws her from the Golden Gate,
And drives her to the Redwoods on a date,
And breaks his trust, commits the seventh sin,
He's plunged into a game he cannot win.
Now broken, half insane he wanders free,
Until by chance he happens on Judy.
And now o'ercome by self-projecting love,
He recreates his fallen, faulty dove,
Until with shock he finds the two the same,
And goes berserk and puts on her all blame.
"You were an apt pupil," crazed he cries;
They mount the stairs, she screams, she falls, she dies.
To heal all this, to show love can be blest,

He turns to Grant and makes NORTH BY NORTHWEST.
Once more the woman caught between two men,
A lightweight ROT, a spy in master den.
But now the selfish male, a knave before,
Reforms and rescues her on Mount Rushmore,
As Mason on the brink sees Leonard fall,
Remarks "Real bullets? not...sporting" are at all.
As Eve and Adam slowly made their way,
And forward looked, not back on Eden's day,
Just so the Fifties struggled not in vain,
And disappeared with lovers on the train.

CANTO X: The Sixties

   As seashores rise and tower o'er the plain,
And mountains sink beneath the briny main,
As puny man 'gainst nature spends his breath,
His only ally art to fend off death,
So change the rule in shifting Hollywood,
Where all that lasts are pictures that are good.
What fifty years of timeless empires sought,
Could within days expire and come to naught;
How once proud lots to real estate return;
How once proud logos bought by foreign firm.
No longer mogul ruled with velvet fist;
Now rose the agent and his actor list.
Gone now the repertory company,
Replaced by deals, enormous actor's fee.
The stars now free could claim a vict'ry won,
Yet each new film must be from scratch begun.
So budgets soared and with them lawyers' fees,
And once mocked moguls's speech turned legalese.
The long despised production code expired,
But scripts dragged on with old conventions tired.
The screen grew big and colorful to see,

Yet substance lacked except for scenery.
And Muse let me not geriatric wail,
The loss of time like Nestor who could rail
Against the Greeks for failure to raze Troy,
Who weren't the men he fought with as a boy.

   All was not lost, though studios were gone;
The lust to look inspired the talent on.
We last saw Stewart stupefied by fates,
When further probed he turns to Norman Bates.
Through MARNIE, BIRDS great Hitch his furies fled,
And showed in age his genius was not dead.
And Ford the lode of meaning still explored,
Summed up the West, the genre he adored.
Wayne shot Lee Marvin, Stewart took the fame;
Wayne died alone as Stewart rose in name.
Such legends grow from rumor's subtle hint,
And we, time's fools, put legends into print,
So law and order based on force we see,
And heroes die so greenhorns can be free.

   Now Wilder Diamond finds to scratch a plot,
And Monroe sings because SOME LIKE IT HOT.
Then Shirley lifts dumb Jack where bosses pee;
He wises up, takes her, reclaims his key.
THE MISFITS film of talents great and woe,
The final takes of Clark and M. Monroe;

He like a king died acting out his part;
She like a victim had no life but art.
Could Hollywood survive the royal stud?
When lo! Paul Newman hustles into HUD.
He wins the nomination for his LUKE,
No statue gains till later, in a fluke.
His wife, Joanne, first garnered picture pride,
When THREE FACED EVE attempted suicide;
What other couple blessed by Hollywood,
Could Oscar's win and keep their marriage good?
Old Randy rides the COUNTRY HIGH once more,
As Peckinpah surpasses Ford in gore.
His WILD BUNCH rob the bank and then the train,
And sacrifice their lives but not in vain.
The Queen of Diamonds triggers captive's will,
Releases brain-washed Harvey's urge to kill,
Until Sinatra slow in slumber wakes,
And foils the dreams' MANCHURIAN CANDIDATEs,
The first of many paranoiac plots,
Where Marx with Freud combat on movie lots.
Kubrick makes STRANGELOVE, comedy too rare,
That mocks the cold war's efforts to prepare;
Atomic doomsday caused by sicko men,
They drop the bomb, we "Don't Know Where or When."
Then HAL takes charge of ship in space employed,

As Strauss's music stirs the hominoid.
   Romantic film grown old since its heyday,
Survives long toothed in Grant and Doris Day.
Rock Hudson, Garner, add their comic charms,
Though Doris suffers outrage in their arms.
A working girl, her virtue seems a void,
When juxtaposed to thought of Sigmund Freud.
Shapiro's scripts concerned with that complex,
Of castrate males made anxious by the sex,
Project onto T. Randall all their fears,
And exorcise themselves as Doris nears.
The male, now shorn, domestic bliss his pay;
Doris herself submits to custom's way.
What difference from the Thirties' films we see,
Though this new love has some equality,
They don't invent themselves as Cavell said,
But rather fate and Freud place them in bed.
   While early Sixties Doris made the queen,
A new male image landed on the screen.
Sean Connery the name; James Bond the part,
The longest series run in filmdom's art.
License to Kill the legend of the spy,
Who outwits KGB and FBI,
Yet transcends Cold War, far below,
And combats evil pure in DR. NO.

Both sides imperiled by wicked schemes of SMERSH,
James Bond's empowered by deft Q's research.
With latest gadgets sets the goons on fire;
And bides his time and toys with his desire.
His license is to kill not to make love,
Yet Bond swings down like Jupiter above,
With villain, agent, victim, he cares not,
Each girl an icy challenge to make hot.
Pussy Galore chose Lesbos as her way,
Until Bond fends her off amidst the hay.
As M, his Dad, exasperated cooks,
While Moneypenny, Mom, adjusts her looks.
Light hearted as he kills, "You've had your six";
Light hearted as he sleeps around for kicks;
So came the revolution's sexual mode,
Before the expiration of the Code.
   From Europe's ashes cinema arose,
And caused embattled Hollywood new woes.
Here was a cinema of life urbane,
Of Neo-Realists and their themes humane:
DeSica, Rosselini first to shine;
Fellini, Antonioni - true sublime!
From colder clime young Bergman parts his seals;
From Britain angry men and Ealing reels;
From France who filmic quality would save,

Achieved that end by letting flow New Wave.
All these new cinemas' revolt,
Made Hollywood look tame and not adult.
The writers ever haters of the Code,
Thought its demise would lift from them a load;
Not morals but profits the producers sought,
Producers who the censorship had wrought,
But now the times demanded something hot;
And censorship itself they 'greed to blot.
Away the Code! Hello the rating games;
G, PG, PG +, and R the names.
Now sex and violence could be fitted in,
With mogul, star, and agent free of sin.
"It's up to you, the audience to choose;
We only rate them, do not share their views."
So graphic sex with graphic death combines,
And blasphemy creeps in between the lines.

   Yet ever when those shifts in taste occur,
And taboos fall as former bound'ries blur,
A vital spark ignites some vital part,
And tired regimes renew their grasp on art.
First fruits of freedom, liberty of race,
And whitest table sets Poitier a place.
Then Hoffman as THE GRADUATE appears,
With Mrs. Robinson, beyond his years.

For such transgressions death the former pay,
But now we laugh the Oed'pal crime away,
And cheer as Dustin struggles toward the church,
Leaves Katharine's groom, like Colbert's, in the lurch.
To New York next as Ratso slum bum gimp,
Inspires Jon Voight to see beyond the limp.
Likewise once tragic lovers on the run,
Transform to BON...AND CLYDE who have such fun,
Who take the Great Depression's poverty,
And treat it as a folklore comedy.
All shocking more the final bloody scene,
As riddled bodies slump across the screen,
And all the jokes, and jivey music tunes,
Cannot reheal the lover-suffered wounds.
For Dunaway, for Beatty stardom nears;
For Parsons critics cry and Oscar cheers;
For Pollard, Wilder, Hackman, new careers.
More shocking than Mike Nichols, Arthur Penn,
Was Houston's GOLDEN EYE on Army men;
More shocking than the EYE were BOB AND TED,
Who CAROL AND ALICE wished to swap in bed.
   Scorcese, Coppola, DePalma rise,
As Altman flies young Brewster's indoor skies;
On Liberty's remains Chuck Heston gapes,
Space travel leads to PLANET OF THE APES;

As FUNNY GIRL brought Barbra from despair;
Paul Newman and Rob Redford made a pair.
The decade ends with motorcycle trip,
When two drugged youths decide it would be hip,
To travel east and ride against the sun,
To share their goods with novice Nicholson;
They wear a flag, the emblem of the free,
Was license killed, or was it liberty?

CANTO XI: The Police State

  O Paradox so seldom understood,
That freedom ushers in some bad with good;
The brainless thought, adopting modern creed,
If code were trashed, the movies would be freed;
But like our parents who from crime awoke,
To find but labor, sweat, and marriage yoke,
So movie makers bit the rating bait,
And found not bliss but cops in fallen state.
  First shot was BULLITT starring Steve McQueen,
With stirring chase through bumpy Frisco scene.
Good men against the bad was nothing new;
What changed? the hero and his point of view.
For now the cop like former private eyes,
Was caught between two gangs of gruesome guys;
The crooks, of course, crazed tripping on their drugs,
But here the cops, the brass, were also thugs.
Without, within, beset from every side,
At work, his friends; at home, his pretty bride;
She married him; she loved his manly force;
Detective work, not play, led to divorce.
Remarried now and in a safer home,

She lets him see the kids, no more his own.
He takes to drink in shabby, messy room,
Befriends the hooker, parallel in gloom.
Within the precinct born; it's here he dies;
Its walls of green the limit of his eyes;
He cannot leave the Force, he can't withdraw;
There is no world beyond this metaphor.
A faithful partner, oft of other race,
Is sure to die or suffer in his place.
The higher ups corrupt, the D.A. too,
It's up to him to justify the Blue.
He punches punks, on civil rights he's low,
Yet never lies and never once takes dough.
Beaten, badgered, blamed from every side,
He saves his worth, integrity, and pride.
With Popeye's FRENCH CONNECTION Hackman stays;
As DIRTY HARRY makes Clint Eastwood's days.
Duke Wayne, one-lunged, portrays the cop McQ,
In BUSTING Gould shows he can trigger too.
Peppard, Burt Reynolds, Scheider, George C. Scott,
Pacino, Russell, Gere, and ROBOCOP,
Mel Gibson, Glover, Douglas, Dennis Quaid,
Morale is low, here's Jamie Lee to aid.
The genre laughs, lets comic actors thrive,
And Eddie Murphy's beat's Rodeo Drive.

While Sellers makes our bellies split in pain,
As daft Clouseau drives Herbert Lom insane.
They solve the crime, reveal the source of woe,
But sit alone, despised, like SERPICO.
Irish or Italian, WASP no more,
The WASP must stoop, as rule he did before;
Polocks, Jews, Hispanics, Blacks are seen,
But WASPs once central now but mar the screen.
WASP actors, yes! they still deserve some fame,
But in these parts they take an ethnic name,
For in this world of paranoid alarm,
The upper class establishment means harm.

   For almost thirty years we've watched this cop;
This urban cowboy's squad car just won't stop.
As if a thousand movies wouldn't suffice,
TV spawned clones, but made MIAMI VICE.
Two other genres serve as cops' ally:
The caper film and disenchanted spy.
Just as the cop between two evils hurled,
So does the robber justify his world.
The bank, corrupt, since days of Robin Hood;
The law, corrupt, and bad has turned from good.
What matter then if thief steals all the loot?
More honest he than frauds in business suit.
No code to foil, to jail he's seldom sent,

If virtue's dead, long live entitlement!
THE THOMAS CROWN AFFAIR the genre forms;
In DOLLARS Richard Brooks outfrisks the norms,
As Warren Beatty, Goldie Hawn outwit,
Goldfinger and Scott Brady with their hit.
As cousin Murray learns his cutting skills,
That lead to COPS and all the "Bad Boy" thrills.
   If copper films reveal the paranoid,
Spy films peer further down the void,
Where both sides err, shown comically in Bond,
Here malice stirs an evil far beyond;
Ideals are lost, no longer can one blame,
What matters else but win the power game?
So deft the machinations, deep the rot,
One loses all one's bearings, and the plot.
Carré began the genre with his SPY
WHO FROM THE COLD CAME IN, but had to die.
In PARALLAX we see a sim'lar VIEW,
Where twists of plot turn all events untrue.
In CONDOR Redford suffers his THREE DAYS;
It matters not who serves or disobeys;
Gene Hackman listens in as lovers walk;
He's driven mad the more he probes their talk.
If film noir favored Freud and psychic depths,
The double agent trods in Kafka's steps.

As fear abroad, so fear torments our home;
Like bombs, reactors threaten their SYNDROME;
And honest Jane, reporter once again,
Risks life and love to thwart misguided men.
   Confined to cells alone the heroes sit;
Gone now romantic love and verbal wit.
The women stripped, upon their breasts we gape,
Descended they from reverence to rape.
All sex is good, with hero, villain, toy;
The woman mounts so we can see her joy.
More macho ever grow the hollow men,
Themselves a zero, look for number **10**.
Instead the nebbish comic question runs:
Is God or Woody Allen number one?
Or is he God, does God exist at all?
Best court Diane and produce ANNIE HALL.
   Go west young fan! but no escape you'll find;
The police state became a state of mind.
Instead of showing how the West was won,
Films now despair of how it was undone.
The noble savage kept his kingdom wild,
And Dustin Hoffman's saved as Indian child.
The white man brought firewater, guns, disease,
Destroyed the plains, the rivers, cut the trees,
Killed all the life from game to Indian tribe,

Built statues to himself and genocide.
BIG MAN reveals the folly Custer made,
A west deemed safe for MILLER AND MCCABE,
A dingy waste, a set on desert built,
For whores and cheats and unrelieved guilt,
Where sound tracks rattle like a snake,
And heroes learn society's a fake.
If Eastwood rides, he rides on through,
A JOSEY WALES disgusted with the view,
And JUDGE ROY BEAN was not the crook he seemed;
He's needed now in West that's unredeemed,
Where Sergeant Tyree runs LAST PICTURE SHOW,
And JUNIOR BONNER's doomed to rodeo.
Though Anglo-Saxon fortunes fail and sag,
Let BRONCO BILLY wave a diverse flag.

   Film noir no longer framed by code,
Gives CHINATOWN and incest à la mode;
While gangster films go epic in parts three;
GODFATHER's lower law: ethnicity.
Freed from the code "reality" holds sway,
Makes MARVIN GARDENS, GYPSY MOTHS, PAYDAY.
Though plots of irony's dark fate abound,
Within their depths some masterworks are found.
RAIN PEOPLE shines with all artistic grace,
As Shirley Knight, with child, tries to escape,

Goes on the road, picks hitcher for a date,
In motel tryst discovers metal plate.
She mothers him, can't leave him on his own,
Till reptile zoo, when Duvall takes her home.
There second tryst turns tragic in the night,
As Flash's daughter "Killer" kills in fright.
Another fav'rite, COMA shares the view,
Of police state as seen by Nancy Drew,
Where residents to women condescend,
And doctors kill to meet financial end;
Unaided by her love or surgeon chief,
She undergoes his knife, the major thief.
In '34 Frank Capra's was the best,
Here madness rules and triumphs CUKOO'S NEST.
These newer visions new directors need;
Scorsese knows where such MEAN STREETS will lead;
DePalma masters cut as Hitchcock's heir,
And betters Stephen King with CARRIE's scare.
Cimino makes the best of Viet War,
With Kubrick SHINING as he had before.
Again, a cop swims counter to the laws,
And Spielberg breaks the surface with his JAWS.
   One cannot blame the sons of Malibu,
For buying up ironic points of view.
The movies' charm had on two bases stood:

New methods linked to old enduring good;
But when film cast out virtue from its ken,
As years before had masters of the pen,
And made the "real" the norm in virtue's place,
It all at once lost any sense of grace;
And human nature pressed in mold this thin,
Flat out professed primeval guilt and sin.
If drama's laws the drama's patrons give,
Blame not the film and flawed executive;
Blame then yourself who patronize such laws,
And hear from Pope from whence derived their cause:
"Philosophy that leaned on Heaven before,
Shrinks to her second cause and is no more;
Religion blushing veils her sacred fires,
And unawares Morality expires."

CANTO XII: Century and Millennium

   Does universal darkness cover all?
O Muse end not with film's decline and fall.
Though fallen sure, on hard days fallen down,
As blasphemy and porno scenes abound,
As shattered glass and bullets spray the lot,
To compensate for total lack of plot;
No miracle of writing can raise up,
The undimensioned ciphers of such stuff;
As sacrifice to confrontation runs,
And foes face off with Tarantino guns,
A random murder leads into the maze,
Each clue a danger to the hero's gaze,
Yet look he will; the end sees no surprise,
The trail led to the paranoid head guys.
Obligatory now the ur'nal scene,
And every star must pee upon the screen.
   Yet mongst the shards new seeds of life appear,
As police state cannot all commandeer.
As clouds of dust raised up by met'ors fall,
Obscured the light and doomed the dinosaur,
While smaller mammals free from terror's jaws,

Adapted well to evolution's laws,
So Hollywood still has its common man,
Whose breath breathed life when Hollywood began.
Fresh ROCKY from South Philly raised his fist;
And ROCKY III shows Rocky what he missed;
Apollo Creed must teach him to get back,
And Rocky learns the virtues of the Black.
No longer Step 'n Fetchit, Beulah parts,
No longer bound to dance and music arts,
The Black too long had more than paid his dues;
At last we see a LADY SING THE BLUES.
As SHAFT hoists up oppression's ling'ring wrong,
SWEET SWEETBACK sings his BAD ASS SONG.
In GLORY Denzel, Morgan show their worth,
Provide new look to war and nation's birth,
And complex urban tragi-comedy,
Does THE RIGHT THING for us, for film, and Lee.
   George Lucas, fresh from S.C.'s movie course,
Goes from GRAFITTI to create "The Force."
Hans Solo's Ford drives Luke into the skies;
There'll be no peace until Darth Vader dies.
From Joseph Campbell Lucas drew his plot;
To Jung and Sarah Lawrence owes a lot;
With sound, effects we see his empire grow,
And Hollywood must north to Marin go.

His good friend Steve retains director's chair,
And seats the ARK in midst of Nazi lair,
And from old heroes fashions up his Jones,
Whose hat and whip belie his search for bones.
He first ENCOUNTERS space of that THIRD KIND,
Then brings E.T., the greatest backyard find,
Who takes his place with Dorothy, Snow White,
And resurrects the movies' magic light.
Steve does it all, as mogul makes his mark,
Breaks all the records with JURASSIC PARK,
But keeps returning back to World War II,
And takes a risk, as Jones himself would do.
Instead of fiction's easy fantasies,
He tests the truth of genocide's disease,
In black and white surveys the Holocaust,
And shows the horror, shows a Nazi boss,
A charlatan? a saint? a fool or knave?
What e'er the cause, mankind's not all depraved.
For which he's blamed, though SCHINDLER Oscars won,
And Spielberg showed his empire's of the sun.
 On genres Hollywood has e'er relied,
And none of them in century's time have died.
Disaster films: eruption, twister, quake;
Computer graphics keep the stunt man safe.
TITANIC sinks, once more it hits the ice;

But raises all the crew to princely price.
The horror movie slasher has become,
Carol Glover says because of single mum;
Though made for boys, the "last girl" copes with heart,
And blasts the TERMINATOR's thousandth part.
In film, as life, we're shocked by Viet War,
And shown more horrors than we've seen before,
More ironies, more treacherous commands,
More stupid waste where sullen RAMBO stands.
DEER HUNTER points the way to film this scene;
In mud and gore we see the PLATOON scream.
GOOD MORNING VIETNAM despite its talk,
Confirms FULL METAL JACKET's deadly walk.
The neo-noirs not quite to noir conform,
More violent they, less subject to reform,
In them no frame of former Code appears,
To restore law as end in chaos nears;
And 'stead of rainy nightmare streets,
The color bakes in desert, tropic heats,
Or winter wastelands spawn unclever cheats.
The nat'ral fool to femme fatale succumbs;
Hurt goes to jail; in hammock Turner suns.
De Niro drives a TAXI, sees a tart,
And triggers shot that nears the nation's heart.
When Michael Douglas has a hot affair,

Glenn Close moves in and makes his wife aware,
And threatens only child on coaster ride,
Until Ann murders her and child inside.
Val Kilmer KILLs... AGAIN and takes a fall,
In debut work of deft director Dahl.
From Arizona north the Coens go,
To let a wife track Macy through the snow.
From FARGO to the South, they do their job,
Then back to noir, the 40s, Billy Bob.
From L.A. past the neo-noirs have strayed,
To L.A.'s future and the RUNNERS BLADE.
   Demented lovers still the nation drive,
as KILLERS, FICTION, ROMANCE stay alive;
And women too escape onto the road;
LOUISE AND THELMA make the truck explode,
And then, now killers, running from the law,
They plunge their car into the canyon's maw.
With so much crime there's little gangster space,
Yet PRIZZI'S HONOR holds a special place.
The West, now lost, by WOLVES and gals o'erun,
Its former heroes villains have become.
   The musical has waned but not expired;
Travolta gave us hope, in dance inspired,
As FEVER mounted, GREASE combined with HAIR,
And DIRTY DANCING heated Catskill air.

The bio long on tuneful melodies,
Adapts itself to age of ironies.
As Patsy Kline takes off in her career,
Too soon at rest her sad SWEET DREAMS we hear.
As Buddy Holly, Gary Busey grins,
While Richy Vallens with LA BAMBA wins;
Together in a plane their songs expire,
As Jerry Lee must cool GREAT BALLS OF FIRE.
  Poor comedy had languished long in pain,
Till TOOTSIE raised its laughing face again,
As Dorothy can Dustin Lange enpal,
While Murray writes "Return to Love Canal."
The son of Parkyourcarkus, Albert Brooks,
Make MODERN ROMANCE, simple in its looks,
Profound in fact, the problem it conveys:
It's not the world, but self that love evades.
In MOONSTRUCK Cher too seldom seen on screen,
Finds Cage a better trap than what had been;
And SLEEPLESS IN SEATTLE wakes to free,
Long dormant second marriage comedy.
Most wakeful of them all was GROUNDHOG DAY,
When Phil the weatherman could have his say,
Create the day whichever way he would,
And freed himself by learning to do good.
The best screenplay since movies had their birth;

How could blind Oscar overlook its worth?
Another miss, a hit that should have been,
Was HERO, which to Capra was akin;
Unlike JOHN DOE whose plot would not resolve,
From off the ledge two heroes can evolve.
Though clerics long have suffered movie scorn,
And to be wicked means to be reborn,
One brave exception counters false report,
Bears witness in that court of last resort,
The audience, who TENDER MERCIES crave,
Applaud a Christian, neither fool nor knave,
Who by God's grace recovers from his fall,
And wins a wife, a son; so wins Duvall.

   Survey the talent scene as century ends,
For film success upon the star depends.
Close, Lange, Sigourney, Pfeiffer, Streep hold sway,
Yet Oscar looks ahead; he sees Tomei.
In MYSTIC PIZZA Julia Roberts cooks,
To doughy men she offers up her looks;
As PRETTY WOMAN prostitutes sans shame,
With BROCKOVICH she earns her Oscar fame.
While Griffith, Melanie has shone since SMILE,
And Madeleine Stowe made STAKE OUT more worthwhile.
As flowers bud, burst into bloom, and die,
So actresses find fame and see it fly;

Though Davis, Crawford, Hepburn broke the laws,
The rest too oft have died at menopause;
So may Winona, free from crime act on,
So may Meg Ryan, Reese, and Cameron,
So may Kate Hudson, child of Goldie Hawn,
Survive among the sexy starlet spawn.
    Among the men, some stand above the ranks,
One thinks of Cruise, and versatile Tom Hanks.
Ed Harris shows a range for different parts,
As do Denzel and Depp in actors' arts,
And Leonardo raised from icy brine,
Escapes THE GANGS and helps the Feds fight crime.
The certain sign an actor is a hit:
Take off his shirt, and show the girls Brad Pitt.
Red Skelton-like Jim Carrey twists the screen,
His humor, puerile, anal, not obscene,
From fluid face his fluid body flows,
Yet act he can, in TRUMAN, Kaufman shows.
Great Britain ever fertile in these lines,
Has offered Hopkins, Daniel Day-, and Fiennes.
   The decade's dean director, Kubrick, fell,
Cut down by time whose cause he served so well.
But one remains who matched his filmic feats,
Now strides alone, above the low MEAN STREETS.
From RAGING BULL to Edith Wharton's AGE,

In which dear Catharine dances center stage,
From TAXI DRIVER to those AFTER HOURS,
NEW YORK, NEW YORK's GOODFELLAS waste their powers,
Scorsese grew, "Life Lessons" he discerned,
In Pantheon, he wears the laurel he earned.
Still on the far side, set to go,
Are Pollack, Badham, Davis, Bigelow,
McTiernan, Scott, who favor macho men,
X-rate Verhoeven, German Petersen.
McBride, Noyce, Jordan, Newell, Mike Leigh,
Mendes and BEAUTY's marred misogyny;
Avnet from BUSINESS, fries, to Warsaw climbs,
Chris Nolan deconstructs MEMENTO's times,
While second Steve, the Soderbergh, lays claim
From Steve the first to snatch fame's mortal flame.
Yet neither one could e'er such laurels gain,
Without the skill of caster Debra Zane.
  As global warming lures the southern birds,
To test their wings amongst more northern herds;
As northern metals draw the compass arms,
So migrant magnet Hollywood still charms,
And from Down Under rise into the sky
New lights to brighten L.A.'s smoggy eye.
First Gibson, Weir, two Hogans, and Sam Neill,
Then sexy Kidman, quick her clothes to peal;

Yet more sublime, fat Muriel's slim Collett,
And best of all uncanny Cate Blanchett,
Who turns a vibrant Liz to regal stone,
Makes foolish Cusack for his crimes atone,
And then gives class to Ripley's phony game,
Her fate, our hope, in Hollywood to reign.
Already king is dour Russell Crowe,
Who from a cop became an emp'ror's foe;
In '47 went to Tiger Town,
Portrayed tormented Nash in cap and gown.

   A century past, a new millennium come,
Did movies ever see what they had done?
Not unaware since first the studio stood,
They often asked the PRICE of HOLLYWOOD.
Of all the fabled films that sought to show,
The underside beneath the glitt'ry glow,
We think of Cukor, Wellman, Judy's spouse,
Yet Altman's PLAYER best portrayed the louse.
How greed and glory, nature's play with art;
How fiction, truth can never be apart;
How false is true, and truth the false reveals;
How justice less than happiness appeals.
Here actors play their parts and play themselves,
As film within the film film history delves.
Ironic yes, but loving all the same.

A comic satire on the movie game.
Such wit and talent ready to command,
Bodes well for future days in movie land.
  Then Muse release me from this task of love!
To wander in the stars with saints above.
Always beset with money worry woes,
Film will survive at least on "pay per" shows,
On VCRs, on cable, shopping malls,
At work, at home on 3-D bedroom walls,
On laser disks, on future holograph,
The art the same, the art of Biograph.
It matters not if Sony's Japan owned,
Of more concern are moguls who get stoned.
Techniques be praised, yet be it understood,
That freedom of the press made Hollywood;
Reporter heroes served as metaphors:
No boss or state could dominate the laws;
That common men could rise and heroes be;
Once lose that common touch: catastrophe.
The same with morals everywhere the same,
Despite the sophists sneering snarling blame.
Let Ozu, Ray, Kiarostami then suffice,
The highest human act is sacrifice.
If film be free from government control,
Though free itself decorum to enroll,

Then Hollywood and movies we shall see,
Will serve the Truth, the Truth that makes them free.
Fear not an age of lead, a fallen space,
The time is ever now and this the place.
Conclusion: Not whatever is, is right,
But look above, transform the world with light.

ABOUT THE AUTHOR

William Park received his BA degree from Princeton and his Ph.D. from Columbia. After teaching at Hamilton College and Columbia, in 1962 he joined the Faculty of Sarah Lawrence College, where, with Wilford Leach, he founded the program in film studies. He is the co-editor of The College Anthology of English and American Poetry and the author of The Idea of Rococo. He has published numerous essays on the novel. His essays on film have appeared in The Hudson Review, The Velvet Light Trap, The Journal of Popular Film, and Crisis. In 1998 he won the Catholic Press Association's award for the "Best Review" of the year. He is the regular film reviewer for the Irish monthly Position Paper. With his wife, Marlene, he now resides in Santa Cruz, California.

www.ingramcontent.com/pod-product-compliance
Lightning Source LLC
LaVergne TN
LVHW091555060526
838200LV00036B/851